PONCA CHIEFS painted by Karl Bodmer

THE PONCA PEOPLE

*by Joseph H. Cash
and
Gerald W. Wolff*

Scientific Editor: Henry F. Dobyns
General Editor: John I. Griffin

PUBLISHED BY INDIAN TRIBAL SERIES / PHOENIX

FELIX W. ALLEN
Chairman, Ponca Tribal Business Committee of Oklahoma

Felix W. Allen was born on the Ponca Reservation on July 18, 1918. His mother was Susie Collins Allen of the Ponca Tribe; his father was John Allen, of the Tonkawa Tribe. Young Felix received his education in the public schools of Tonkawa, Oklahoma. On July 25, 1940, Mr. Allen married Lorraine Hinman, daughter of Richard and Margaret D. Hinman of the Ponca Tribe. They had seven children, five girls and two boys.

v

During World War II Mr. Allen served with the Seventh Infantry Division, which was credited with destroying over 60,000 Japanese soldiers. Mr. Allen was one of the first American soldiers to recapture United States territory, landing in the first wave at Holtz Bay on Attu Island on May 11, 1943, and Lilly Creek on Kiska Island on August 15. On February 2, 1944, Jr. Allen participated in the landing on Kwajalein in the Marshall Islands, and on October 20 he landed on the Leyte Island beachhead when General Douglas MacArthur fulfilled his view to return to the Philippines. This Ponca warrior landed in the first wave of assault troops on Okinawa on April 1, 1945.

During the battle for Okinawa, Mr. Allen suffered severe combat injuries. These led him to retire early from his employment in the Commercial Division of Cessna Aircraft Co., in Wichita, Kansas, in October, 1964. Mr. Allen belongs to the American Legion and the Veterans of Foreign Wars, the Methodist and Native American Churches. As Chairman of the Ponca Tribal Business Committee, he brought to a climax and per capita pay out on April 3, 1975, the award to the Ponca Tribe made by the U. S. Indian Claims Commission.

Ponca Tribal Business Committee Chairman Felix W. Allen dedicates this book to

DONALD ALLEN (ATAHOCK)

In memory of his son, who was killed in line of duty on June 8, 1972, while stationed at Fort Davis, Panama Canal Zone.

Donald Allen was born to Felix W. Allen and Lorraine H. Allen on June 3, 1952. He received his elementary education in Wichita, Kansas, public schools. He graduated from Riverside Indian School, Anadarko, Oklahoma, in May, 1971. On July 27, Donald Allen enlisted in the U. S. Army Paratroops.

They are an old people, but they learned to live in a new world. They were a people of rivers who could function well on the high plains. They were a people of the north who were removed at a late time to the south. They were a horticultural people who could also hunt the buffalo. They were a people of peace who could fight as well as anyone in defense of their lands and their tribe. They were, and are, the Poncas — a people who survived.

THE ORIGINS OF THE PONCA

Ponca means "sacred head" and is the name of the outstanding group of people who comprise one of the most courageous and sensible of all American Indian tribes. The Poncas are part of the Siouan linguistic family and speak Dheghia, which is a division of that large language group. This particular grouping includes the Poncas themselves, their close relatives the Omahas, the Osages, the Kansas, and the Quapaw. The Ponca dialect is the same as that of the Omaha and very similar to that of Quapaw.

As was true of all the Siouan tribes, their origins are shrouded in the mists of time. We can be certain they were in the Ohio Valley around 1500 A.D. There is a strong school of thought that suggests that they originated in the Carolina and Virginia Piedmont region and moved from there to the Ohio area. Another theory is that their earliest origins were in the Ohio Valley where they eventually divided, some going to the southeast and others to the west and the northwest.

It is almost certain that the five groups comprising the Dheghia language group were united at one time. In about 1500, all five lived in the area around the Ohio and Wabash rivers, and it was at about that time that they separated. They all journeyed downstream to the Mississippi. The first division, the Quapaw, followed the Mississippi down to the Arkansas River. The Omaha and the others traveled north. The Osages soon split from the others and went to what is now the Osage River in Missouri. The Kansas moved up the Missouri a short distance. The Omaha went still further north into the general area between Omaha, Nebraska and Sioux City, Iowa. The Ponca, still closely associated with the Omaha, traveled farthest into the north country, establishing themselves in the area drained by the Niobrara River, which enters the Missouri across and slightly above the present-day town of Springfield,

2

South Dakota. They built their major village at the mouth of the Niobrara, but they established other settlements as well.

In their trek to the north — while they were still with the Omaha — the Ponca lived for a short time in the Iowa area and apparently ranged as far north as the pipestone quarry at Pipestone, Minnesota. There is some evidence that they had a village there. They left Minnesota when the Yankton Dakota moved into the region, and apparently the Ponca separated from the Omaha in the vicinity of the James River in South Dakota and migrated west of the Missouri River. There is also evidence that about 1650 they ranged as far west as the Black Hills. It is certain that they were on the Niobrara in 1673, and it is also certain that during this period they somehow managed to arrange for peaceful relations with the Lakota of the west and the Yanktons of the east. This arrangement, while it occasionally ruptured, remained basically unchanged until the middle of the 19th century.

The Ponca lived in earth lodges in rather tightly structured villages. Their lifestyle resembled that of Arikaras and Mandans, who were also dwellers along the Missouri. The Ponca built their earth lodges around a four-post arrangement with lintels supporting the heavy, igloo-shaped outside structure. The lodges were difficult to construct, but they provided great protection from the terrible heat of the summers and the awful cold of the winters on the northern Plains. The Poncas protected their villages with cottonwood log stockades to prevent raiders from entering without a fight.

The Ponca people subsisted mainly on horticultural products. They grew corn, squash, pumpkins, beans, and other commodities in small fields along the Niobrara, Ponca Creek and Missouri River bottomlands. They also did considerable fishing. In addition, they conducted periodic hunts on the Plains and were known to have killed buffalo in considerable numbers even before they acquired horses. They did this by maneuvering the buffalo into a position where they could be stampeded over a cliff or down a steep hill, which would cause large numbers of the ungainly beasts to pile up and expire. Prior to the acquisition of the horse, this process — known as buffalo-jumping — was the most certain Ponca method of insuring a large supply of meat and hides.

When they hunted, the Poncas used that most typical of Plains Indian habitations, the tipi. They erected tipis around a basic structure of three poles, which the women set up in perfect balance. More poles would then be added to insure strength, stability, and the desirable structure. Then the whole pole frame would be covered with a tent cover made of sewn, supple buffalo hides. The tipi included a venting system. By "raising the skirts" of the structure, the occupants regulated the amount of wind, and thus the heat, and made it the most perfect of tents. It provided fresh air and coolness in the summer and warmth in the winter. It could be disassem-

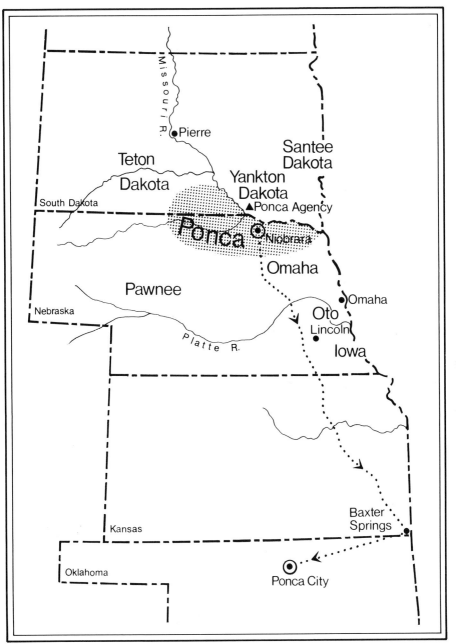

MAP 1. The Ponca Migration.

bled with surprising speed and reassembled nearly as quickly by the women experts.

The Poncas, who lived in relative peace, were among the more kind, generous and agreeable people on the Great Plains. They had achieved an enviable balance with nature. They hated no one, and no one hated them. At the same time, they feared no one. They fought when they had to, but preferred to follow peaceable pursuits. They obtained the horse by the middle of the 18th century, which allowed them to hunt buffalo much more successfully, and insured a greater supply of meat in their diet. Nonetheless, the horse did give greater mobility to their potential enemies and made their life a trifle more dangerous. Likewise, the use of horses tended to lure the Poncas into roaming farther and farther in their hunts, thus exposing their hunters and warriors to greater dangers than had been true in the past.

THE PONCA BANDS

The Poncas camped in a definite order. When the whole tribe gathered, it formed a camp circle with the entrance facing east. The band called the *Wah-jah-ta*, whose duty it was to guard the entrance and check the people going in and out, camped on the left of the opening. The *Wah-jah-ta* had the responsibility of finding anyone who was lost. Inasmuch as they were expert trackers, this was a logical assignment for them. Next to them in the circle were the *Ni-kah-pah-schna*, who were experts on how the human head should be dressed. The third band were the

6

A PONCA VILLAGE painted by Karl Bodmer

this pattern were the mores that made the Poncas beautifully balanced and allowed their survival. They all believed in the same god; they did not kill each other or steal from one another; they stressed kindness. They were against gossip and despised the person who lacked generosity. Perhaps above all, every Ponca had respect for the sacred pipe.

The sacred pipe came into the Poncas' possession after they had come north. They moved into the area of Pipestone, Minnesota, and while living there found the peculiar type of stone called catlinite, which for all the Plains Indians proved to be the ideal material for pipe making. When quarried, it is soft and easily worked, but after exposure it hardens, so it provided the perfect material needed. When the Poncas first saw the red stone, the head chief told them to dig it out and to make a pipe, and this was done. The stem was made later in Nebraska from ash. Through the years, the pipe was apparently lost, and no one is certain where it is today.

STRANGE AND WONDERFUL ANIMALS

The Poncas were wont to leave their villages and go on buffalo hunts up the Missouri and to the west. It was said that they would go as far as the Rocky Mountains to Pike's Peak and then would come back to Nebraska across the plains. Their legends state that south of the Niobrara River they saw a dead elephant and also a prehistoric hairy elephant, which had a long body, forked feet, yellow hair, and was about forty feet long. This animal was said to be alive and

Photograph by Joseph Cash

VIEW OF TWIN BUTTES, near Naper, Nebraska, where Ponca legend says an elephant (mammoth ?) was once seen.

was observed going into its lair near Verdel, Nebraska. Apparently the animal would go into its hole on the coldest days of the winter.

Up the Niobrara River, there were old villages. One was southwest of the Twin Buttes, near the present town of Naper, Nebraska. Close to the Twin Buttes were the forks of the Keyapaha and the Niobrara rivers. The Twin Buttes are still landmarks in the region and are noted for the proliferation of rattlesnake dens on both of them and in the general vicinity. For the Poncas, the buttes were places where their holy men performed ceremonies. On the east butte, it is said that they saw the caves wherein dwelled an elephant.

SPORTS AND GAMES

The games and sports of almost all tribes on the Northern Plains bore a certain similarity. Many of them, or at least their variations, were played by nearly all tribes. In addition, many of these games possessed religious significance and certainly religious powers were brought to bear in order to assure victory to one player or side as opposed to another.

Two of the basic sports were foot racing and horse racing. The foot races represented what is possibly the oldest and most basic sport practiced by mankind. Even these races could have religious significance, as there was usually a ceremonial foot race in connection with the Ponca sun dance. The people gambled a great deal on horse races. They also used several medicines in order to make a horse run faster. Ponca historian Peter LeClaire described the use of the root *Po-ip-iye*, which the race horse owner would chew while he was talking to his horse. This was supposed to be done in secret prior to a race. The owner would keep chewing and telling the horse that it was going to win. He would spit a little of the chewed root on his hands and rub the horse down talking all the while. As the owner rubbed the horse's tail, the last part to be approached, he would tell the animal that its tail would be in the air during the race. LeClaire stated that this particular owner always used this method and always won the races, but disliked it, because he thought it was not entirely fair to the other contestants. Other Poncas mentioned that the mescal buttons, or peyote, were sometimes ground up and given to race horses to make them go faster. Without a jockey club or racing commission, this sort of practice was allowed, and apparently no one objected, because anyone with the knowledge and the power could do it.

The Indian game called shinny was very popular and, like the other games, was religious in nature. A custodian was always appointed to run the shinny game and to keep the sacred ball used in it. He also scheduled the games and announced their dates. The Poncas only played shinny in the spring and, from a practical standpoint, this was probably because it gave the members of the tribe an opportunity to loosen up after an inactive winter. Any man in the tribe could participate if he was able in the four games played every spring.

14

The game was very similar to field hockey and the sticks that were used were usually about three feet long with a curved end. The ball was made of deerskin stuffed with horse hair. The Poncas every year used a new one marked with certain designs that had significance. The major difference between the Ponca shinny game and modern field hockey was that the field itself was a mile long and half a mile wide with a goal post six feet tall at each end of the concourse. The play was fast, tough, and hard, and resulted in an incredible number of barked shins, knotted heads, and split fingers. A team scored a goal when the ball reached an opponent's goal post, and, when one team scored four goals, the game was over.

In the game, certain players seemed to have an advantage because of their medicine bundles. Some Poncas were sure that these bundles gave the players good luck, and stated that they used them every time they played. Others believed that simply touching the ball would cure stiffness. In addition to the men's contest, there was a similar game played only by women. Apparently, there was no integration in the Ponca sports.

The Poncas also developed a very popular dice game played with plum stones. The combination of marks that turned up after the stones were tossed indicated the winner. This pastime was somewhat similar to some modern dice games. The moccasin game, on the other hand, bore a strong similarity to what is known as the shell game. A player from one side would hide a stone under one of four moccasins while singing to distract the opposition. A member of the other side would then attempt to guess the location of the stone. Similar to this was the hand game, which is played by almost all Indians and is still popular with both the Southern and Northern Poncas as well as the Sioux. In this game, two players on one side would hide two pieces of bone or the like in their hands, while a member of the opposite side attempted to guess where they were. Again, even this form of amusement had religious implications, and the implements used in the game were frequently buried with their owner. It is certain that there was considerable gambling involved with much of this entertainment, and that large amounts of personal property often changed hands as a result. In almost all the Ponca games, there were versions played by boys who were, in reality, learning to become men. The Indian youths practiced with enthusiasm and became very skillful by the time they became warriors.

The Ponca games were, in one sense, almost essential psychological diversions for a tense and insecure people who gladly constructed their own forms of amusement to fill the few periods of leisure that they could find in their lives. As a generally merry, hospitable, and gregarious people, the Ponca also genuinely enjoyed all these contests for their own sake and had a good time watching as well as participating in them. Games and sports can be part of the social glue that holds a society together. Certainly modern sport, even in its highly com-

16

mercialized and organized forms, serves that purpose in the United States. This may have been even more the case in the narrow societies of the Poncas, which provided their own brand of organized amusements. In a situation and a life fraught with danger, games and sports helped a people retain sanity and balance. As such they were extremely valuable.

THE OLD RELIGION

In the old days, the Ponca religion revolved around a belief in one god, named *Wakanda*. The Ponca concept was in no way dissimilar from God, as used in the Judeo-Christian sense of the word. Poncas prayed to and worshipped *Wakanda*. They performed ceremonies in his honor and to gain his favor. They gave thanks unto him. In addition to *Wakanda*, Poncas developed the term *Wakanda-Pezi*, which means Satan, after the Poncas learned of Satan from the white men. Being an adaptable people, they took up the idea and developed it for their own usage. The main people who prayed were the chiefs. To be a chief among the Poncas meant that one was automatically a religious leader in the Ponca theocracy. They did not develop a priesthood to the extent that most other Indian tribes on the Plains did.

Experts have labeled the Ponca view of the supernatural as animistic, in that things, places, people, and the like were all capable of possessing supernatural power to one degree or another. The name for this power was *xúbe*. Anything or anyone that had

17

this power was *xúbe*, and anyone who could control it was likewise *xúbe*. *Xúbe* is what the white men mistakenly called "medicine."

One of the ways the Ponca male achieved *xúbe* was by going on a vision quest. One normally sought a vision at the beginning of puberty for it signified both a searching for power and an entrance into manhood. The candidate seeking this power had his face blackened so that everyone could recognize him as a supplicant. He went alone to a hilltop, where he would fast and pray for four days and four nights, taking in only a little food and broth, which was brought to him at night by an older man. If he were sincere, and prayed hard enough, and if he were worthy, the spirit of *xúbe* would manifest itself to him through an animal or a bird. Later in life, he might go on other vision quests in order to get more power, or he could dance a sun dance for the same purpose. *Xúbe* could be purchased in the form of bundles or medicine packets from people who possessed it. This was not considered to have the full power that the individual had received by himself, but it was better than nothing. Sometimes a poor unfortunate would go on more than one vision quest and would come up with nothing. No spirit would manifest itself to him. No vision of any consequence would appear before his fevered eyes. In such a case, purchase was the only solution.

The boy coming down from the mountain brought with him certain objects that related to his vision. They might include a feather, an oddly-shaped rock, a piece of a plant, the skin of a bird, and many other things. These would be placed in a small bag, which would usually be tied around the neck of the owner. Clans or the tribe as a whole also could have medicine bundles. On some occasions, individuals who had never seen a vision even had bundles. These bundles could, in some cases, relate to war and contain scalps. The leader of the war party opened them in order to conjure up directions for a forthcoming battle. Still others could be employed in curing the sick, in hunting, and the like. A few were used to wreak harm on one's individual enemies, but such bundles and such usage were considered dangerous.

Many things had power. The warrior, Whiteshirt, had a war bonnet made of pelican feathers that had *xúbe*. Broken Jaw, a Northern Ponca chief, possessed a bundle that contained a muskrat skin and a wooden paddle. This was used to cure the sick.

The most powerful bundle contained the tribal pipe of the Ponca and is now kept in a special room in the home of the Keeper. Because this pipe has such immense power, the room is in a continual haze or a fog. During the annual Southern Ponca powwow, the pipe is hung above the door of a special tipi. Clans likewise have their own pipes, which are special, and which also have great *xúbe* — but none has the power of the tribal pipe.

Much of the Ponca religious activity centered on the dances and ceremonies that were held periodically. These were very important and consumed a great portion of the male Ponca's time. Three major dances the Sun Dance, typical of all the Plains tribes, the Pipe Dance, and the War Dance — all had special purposes. All of them had great power. Poncas used the Sun Dance in particular to bring rain, which was highly important on the Plains. Although there were other tribal dances, as well as those conducted by societies and cults, the three mentioned above remained basic to the Poncas' ties with the supernatural and with nature for as long as they stayed in their northern homeland. A combination of removal from familiar surroundings and the onslaught of the 20th century diminished the use of the old religion, although the dances that were part of it still continue.

THE PONCA CHIEFS

The Poncas have a long and distinguished history as a separate tribe. They can trace the ancestry of their chieftainship farther back than most of the Indians living on the Great Plains. Tradition says that around 1800 Chief Little Bear was the head chief of the Poncas and remained so until his death in about 1830. He was in turn succeeded by his son, Iron Whip, who was chief until 1870. When Iron Whip, who had signed the treaties of 1858 and 1865, died, the leadership passed to White Eagle, who led the full bloods during the removal to Oklahoma and continued as the head chief until 1914. White Eagle was the key figure in both the transition from the north to the south and in that period when

20

WHITE EAGLE, PONCA CHIEF who led the tribal transition into the 20th century.

the great changes took place in the lifestyle of the Poncas. White Eagle died in 1914 of pneumonia caused from exposure; the old chief had started walking home from the agency and was found nearly frozen to death. He was almost ninety years of age at the time of his death. He in turn was succeeded by his son, Horse Chief Eagle, who held the position until his death. Horse Chief Eagle was the last of the Ponca head chiefs. Adamantly opposed to the new life, he refused to learn English and never spoke to the white man except through an interpreter. He believed very strongly in maintaining the traditions of his people, their secrets, and their ceremonies. In a sense, he was a throwback to the mid-19th century. In another sense, he was the magnificent man standing alone, or nearly so, in the face of the 20th century. Such men are rare and should be cherished.

The Ponca hereditary system of chieftainship provided them with stability of leadership in a period when little else was stable. The length of the rule by each chief indicates that they were men of ability, who by and large satisfied their people. If they had not, they would have been replaced one way or another. Fortunate is any nation that can be led as well for so long a time.

THE STRATEGIC SITUATION OF THE PONCAS

The Ponca people occupied a geographic position that was both difficult and unusual. Their homeland, although situated on the banks of the Missouri and the Niobrara rivers, extended widely to the west,

22

south, and north. It was an area that the Poncas could not wholly settle, yet were required to defend with very few numbers. While the people were not militant, they became warlike when attacked and fought hard to defend their territory and their privileges.

The eastern boundary of the Ponca territory ran roughly from the west bank of the Missouri, opposite the present-day Sioux City, Iowa, down to the mouth of the Platte River. Directly across the river from this boundary were the Omahas, the Poncas' closest friends, allies, and relations. The Omahas hunted west into Ponca country but did so as guests of the Ponca people. The North Platte River formed the southernmost boundary of the Poncas. Directly south of that boundary lived the Pawnees who traditionally hunted to the south, although they would eventually penetrate to the north. The Poncas were, at times, at war with the Pawnees and at other times at peace. Most of the time, the situation had elements of both and this created much anxiety for both groups. The western boundary of Ponca territory was not clearly defined. It apparently ended somewhere west of the Black Hills, and some informants have argued that it even included Pike's Peak in Colorado. This latter boundary would require a Ponca hunting party to go a very long way and would be extremely dangerous, as it would require penetration of Sioux, Arapahoe, and Cheyenne territory. Any one of these tribes was infinitely stronger than the Poncas and one must assume that the Poncas

23

seldom stretched their claims that far west. To the north, the boundary went from the mouth of the White River in South Dakota straight west to the Black Hills. This boundary was severely contested by the Brule division of the Teton Sioux, and, whenever the Poncas penetrated too far north of Ponca Creek, they probably encountered considerable danger. In addition to this, they were wont to cross the river and to hunt along the western edges of Bon Homme and Charles Mix counties in South Dakota. They had done this prior to the arrival of the Yanktons and apparently continued the practice through some sort of diplomatic arrangement with the Yankton people after they arrived in the area.

In addition to the tribes previously mentioned, the Poncas had contact with others at one time or another in their history. To the southwest of them, in an early period, lived the tribe the Poncas called the Padouca. The Poncas identified this people as being the northern elements of the Comanches, but others indicate they may very well have been Lipan Apaches. Whenever the Poncas met this tribe, there was almost instantaneous warfare, which continued until the Padouca finally moved farther to the south.

In the long run, the Oglala and Brule Lakota became the major threats to the Poncas. They had numbers, mobility, and desire. Other Indian groups, who presented no particular problem, moved into the area shortly before the Poncas left. Among these were the Santee Dakota who had been moved from Minnesota following the Uprising of 1862 and had

24

been given a reservation adjacent to that of the Northern Ponca. In addition, the Winnebago Indians from Minnesota had been removed from that state as a result of the same uprising. They went to Crow Creek in South Dakota and then south to what would eventually become a new reservation adjacent to that of the Omahas. In both cases, the Poncas got along well with the newcomers during the short period they were together and the good relationships continued when the Northern Poncas returned.

It should be stressed that the Poncas were not offensive fighters. They did not, as a rule, raid their enemies, nor did individual Poncas seek particular war honors, unless these were thrust upon them. Some raids, of course, were conducted. They were the sole responsibility of the individual who led them, and he was strictly accountable for the results. They were not a matter of tribal policy.

Even so, the main way for a young man to advance was by military success. The warrior's dancing societies emphasized military virtues and encouraged youths to demonstrate their valor in battle. Some men swore never to run during any battle and to die where they stood by anchoring themselves in place. The successful warrior won feathers and other decorations as well as special privileges. Yet, for the Poncas, the military side of life was not as important as it was for the Sioux, the Comanches, and the Cheyenne, who made warfare very nearly a lifestyle. The Poncas fought when they had to fight and usually for good reasons which were connected with

25

the defense and sustenance of the tribe as a whole. This was one of the principal reasons they were able to survive in an impossible strategic situation with inferior numbers.

CONTACT WITH THE WHITE MAN

Although Father Jacques Marquette had seen the Poncas, the European contacts that extend to the present began in 1789, when Jean Monier came up the Missouri from St. Louis. The Upper Missouri and all of Louisiana was at that time in the hands of Spain. France had lost the French and Indian War to England in the 1760's, and, rather than cede Louisiana to the victor, had transferred it to Spain with the idea that it would be easier to recover. This expectation was fulfilled when Napoleon Bonaparte became First Consul of France. During the period of Spanish control, the fur trade remained in the hands of Frenchmen. Spain exercised nominal sovereignty but the Frenchmen were on the spot and knew the business. During this period, St. Louis really developed as a fur trading capital. In need of money, the Spaniards eventually decided that the Upper Missouri was the proper region to explore. Thus the Spanish government and French fur traders combined to send various individuals up the river, and the first to ascend it as far as the Poncas was the aforementioned Monier. He was not to be the last. In any case, when Monier reached the Poncas' fortified village at the mouth of the Niobrara, he traded some, talked a lot, and returned. The very next year Jacques

26

Courtesy of Morrow Collection

PONCA INDIAN WARRIOR

D'Eglise obtained a license which permitted him to hunt on the Missouri. He went up the river and also saw and talked to the Poncas, although he continued into what is now North Dakota, where he met the Mandans. D'Eglise, an ambitious man, wanted to secure a monopoly on the fur trade on the Upper Missouri, but he failed to do so. He did, however, convince the Spaniards that trading was dangerous and was likely to become more so as British representatives were moving into the Dakota Country from Canada.

In 1793, a group of St. Louis merchants and traders formed a company "for the trade and commerce which may, now or in the future, be had with tribes who lived farther up than the Poncas, who are located on the upper part of the Missouri, and in other places in which trade may be carried on." They wanted exclusive trading privileges for ten years, and they called themselves "a company of explorers of the Upper Missouri." They obtained the approval they wanted, and the Spaniards hoped that they were on the way to establishing a trade monopoly with the Mandans and to ousting British subjects from Louisiana. In addition, they felt that they could perhaps discover the source of the Missouri and penetrate as far as the Pacific Ocean. It was indeed an ambitious company, and it was bound to affect the Poncas. In fact, the Ponca village at the mouth of the Niobrara seemed to be the designated jumping-off spot for the majority of its trade.

Jacques Clamorgan headed the Missouri company

with a number of prominent St. Louis merchants as partners. They placed the first expedition they sent in charge of a young French Canadian, Jean Baptiste Trudeau, who was a distant relative of the Lieutenant Governor of Illinois. Trudeau moved up the stream in 1794. D'Eglise, who had already been up the Missouri and back twice, stayed independent of the company. He wanted to trade upriver ahead of Trudeau, and passed him. Trudeau, a newcomer to the river, moved very slowly, because, to be quite frank, he was afraid of Indians. He left St. Louis on June 7 and did not reach the Ponca village until September 14. There he succeeded in sneaking by and did not even talk to the Poncas on his trip north, but he never passed the Mandans. Instead, he decided to move to the south, and, on November 11, Trudeau built a cabin on the east bank of the Missouri River in what is now Charles Mix County, South Dakota. This cabin was the first home erected by a white man in South Dakota and is usually called "Pawnee House," although there is very little doubt that Trudeau intended it to be called "Ponca House." Trudeau traded extensively with the Poncas and other tribes and in 1796 brought back furs to St. Louis.

In the spring of 1795, Clamorgan sent another expedition up the Missouri to join Trudeau. This expedition succeeded in something that few white men have ever accomplished; they made the Poncas angry. So the Poncas blocked the river and forced the expedition to retreat. Yet a third expedition left in

1795 under James Mackay. He started so late that he wintered with the Omahas slightly above the mouth of the Platte and made contact with the Poncas in that manner. Mackay returned in 1797. By this time, the Spaniards had explored enough on the Upper Missouri to know where they were going, and they had a fair idea of the tribes in the area. By 1800, Loisel's post was founded many miles above the Poncas. Trade by that time was fairly constant, and the Poncas learned much about the strange white men and established good and profitable relations with them. It is true that the Poncas were not in the best fur trading area, but they did do some trapping and sold a considerable number of hides. In addition, they were able to trade their garden produce, or at least their small surplus, to the fur traders. The white men came to admire the Poncas as an honorable, peaceful, handsome, and moral people. Such qualities were not always ascribed to Indian tribes by the rough-and-ready fur traders.

In 1800, Spain was forced to cede Louisiana back to France, which kept it until Bonaparte, playing his usual cagey game, suddenly sold it to the United States. Suddenly, the rules and ownership changed. The Poncas, although they could not as yet foresee it, faced their greatest long-range challenge — a challenge that would eventually force them to leave their homeland and greatly altered their lifestyle. The United States President, Thomas Jefferson, sent forth the famous expedition led by Meriwether Lewis and William Clark. The Lewis and Clark group, coming up the Missouri River, received its only casualty in the vicinity of what is now Sioux City, Iowa. The explorers camped a little above the mouth of the Niobrara River at a place that came to be known as Lewis and Clark Point on September 4, 1804. They saw the Poncas, met them, and found them living in the same location where they had been for years before, certainly as long as white men had known them. They also found a tribe that was greatly decimated. The Poncas, who had numbered an estimated 800 in 1780, had been reduced to approximately 200 people by this time. They had been ravaged by a smallpox epidemic, which had also decimated their cousins the Omahas during the winter of 1800-1801. Two hundred people on the northern plains is not many. Yet, they held on, planted their crops, and survived to eventually rebuild their numbers and their strength. Almost alone among the river tribes, they did not particularly blame the white men for the epidemic, even though the Americans had brought them the disease — for which they had little immunity and no cure.

The "Poncars," as Lewis and Clark called them, took the famed explorers for some side trips and showed them the land. The expedition leaders were amazed by the beauty of the country and the abundance of game, and they were most reluctant to leave the camps of the friendly Poncas. Thus, they stayed for some time. Here they heard legends from the older Indians who told them that they had formerly lived by the pipestone quarries but had been driven out by the Sioux. They said that they had once been part of a large tribe, which had been annihilated by their enemies. They had lived on the banks of the Red River of the north and had frequently visited Lake Winnipeg, but the pressure from the Sioux had forced them down to the Missouri and then across it and down to the mouth of Ponca Creek and eventually to their site at the mouth of the Niobrara. At the time Lewis and Clark visited them, their chief was named Smoke, and his sub-chief was called Pure Chief. Both predicted that the tribe would die out, because the buffalo were being killed and hunting was becoming very difficult. Other famous men saw the Poncas as well. George Catlin, the famed artist, visited them and painted them. Carl Bodmer, traveling up the river with his master, Prince Maximillian of Wied, also painted the Poncas.

They were indeed a threatened people. The Sioux, the Osage, the Pawnees, and the Kiowas raided them sporadically. Yet, during this time, they succeeded in consolidating their hold over what is now Knox and Boyd counties in Nebraska and portions of Gregory County in South Dakota. They possessed fine agricultural land, good grazing areas, and an abundance of water. This was an ideal homeland.

In 1817, the government of the United States began a program to secure the loyalty and friendship of the tribes of the Upper Missouri. The War of 1812 had shown the Americans that the Indians had as much loyalty to England as to them. On June 25,

1817, William Clark and August Choteau, acting as commissioners for the United States, signed a treaty of perpetual peace and friendship with the "Poncarar" tribe. The interpreter for the treaty negotiations was Joseph LaFlesche, whose descendants would play an important role in later Ponca history. On June 9, 1825, the Poncas signed still another treaty, this time with Brigadier General Henry Atkinson and Major Benjamin O'Fallon, Indian agent. In the treaty, the Poncas recognized the supremacy of the United States, and the United States promised to protect the Poncas. There were provisions for the regulation of trade and further stipulations that laws should be in the hands of the United States or the tribe, rather than under the control of private individuals. The Poncas further agreed to deliver up any criminal for whom the United States asked. Thus the treaty-making process formalized the relationship of the new nation to the Indian tribe.

At the same time, other relationships continued. The Frenchmen kept trading. Wherever a Frenchman traded, he intermingled and frequently married. Famous French names such as Primeaux, LaPointe, LaFlesche, and LeClaire began to appear among the Ponca people and in time would predominate. At the same time, Poncas intermingled considerably with the Omahas and the Yankton Sioux, who ranged across the river. The Poncas became a nation of mixed bloods earlier than most and the process seemed to produce vitality rather than weakness.

For all of this, the Poncas were a people undergoing considerable change. The coming of the fur traders — with their powder, muskets, axes, and the like — put trade goods at a premium. So the Poncas more and more became buffalo hunters and fur trappers. They were also becoming allies of the Yankton and Teton Sioux and actually fought with them against the Pawnees. One authority suspects that this was because the alliance was one of their few means of self-preservation. They were a small tribe and so felt compelled to form an alliance with the powerful Teton Sioux, while the Pawnees were weaker and could be fought off. There were even occasions when the Sioux forced the Poncas to help them raid the Omaha, who were their closest relatives and friends.

The raiding by the Dakota and Pawnee became part of a pattern that was easily discernible in the Northern Great Plains. The hard-riding buffalo hunting tribes had a preponderance of numbers and military force. They were better armed, better trained, and more experienced in battle than the Poncas. They had the advantage of always being able to attack a foe who was in a fixed location. In other words, they always knew where the Poncas were and how many of them were there to defend their site. They could hit and run. A small Dakota war party quite easily picked off any straggling Ponca hunter or farmer and then rode out on the Plains, where pursuit was too dangerous. All the tribes that lived in

34

ANTONE, Chief of Ponca half-breeds.

villages along the rivers had this problem; from the Mandans, Arikaras, and Hidatsas in the north, to the Pawnees, Omahas, and Poncas to the south, the same thing happened repeatedly. It continued in the case of the Poncas until they were removed to Oklahoma in 1877. The result was that the tribe lived in constant fear and nervousness. Poncas could never leave their stockaded village with any sense of security. Insecurity, in turn, led to psychological problems that perhaps forced hasty and ill-chosen decisions on some occasions.

The Poncas also continued to meet with white men who became more of a problem as time went on. This did not turn out to be the case, when, in 1846, the Poncas were startled to see a small group of Mormons entering their territory. This group had actually been invited to come by some Poncas who were visiting Pawnees near the site of present-day Genoa, Nebraska. The Mormons, whom the Poncas called "Monmona," were provisioned by their hosts and given a camping spot near the camp. They got along very well. According to the Poncas, it was almost a festival of friendship. In the spring, the Mormons decided to leave to join their brethren in Zion, and the Poncas showed them the best route to travel.

The fights with other Indians, however, continued. In 1855, a large-scale battle with the Pawnees took place during the annual buffalo hunt of both tribes. This confrontation, which was technically a Ponca victory, caused great trouble in the long run. Both the Poncas and the Pawnees felt terribly insulted as a result of this battle, and their enmity, which had been sporadic in the past, became a permanent fixture for as long as the two tribes remained in contact.

By the mid-1850's, the Poncas were experiencing severe military and economic difficulties. True, their numbers had revived, but their strategic situation had worsened. The attacks of the hostile plains buffalo hunters multiplied. Ponca security was thus lessened, and the dangers to their survival increased. The buffalo hunt of 1855 proved to be the last successful large-scale hunt they would ever conduct in the north. Poncas would continue to go out, but in smaller parties running much greater risks. They became fearful. As the hunting became less of a source of food, Poncas logically tried to expand their agriculture, but failed. Again, the raids of other tribes made them afraid to plant and cultivate fields very far from the safety of the village and thus prevented this essential expansion of their food supply. From a people who had been prosperous and well-fed, the Poncas were now reduced to periodic starvation, and, as a result, they came to blame the United States for not protecting them. The Poncas reached such a desperate condition that in 1857-58 they destroyed the Niobrara Sawmill and stole items from the government storehouse. This may have made them feel somewhat better, but it did not change their strategic disadvantages.

The government of the United States had known about and dealt with the Poncas for a long time. Americans liked the Poncas; the people were peaceful, industrious, hard-working, and pleasant to be with. Poncas presented no particular problems for the government until the mid-1850's. It is a sad commentary upon the government of the United States that it did not respond as well to peaceful tribes as it did to those that were warlike. The federal government tended to ignore friendly people like the Poncas and lavish money, trade goods, and attention on tribes that were — from the standpoint of the United States — a danger and a threat. Here was truly a case of "the squeaking wheel getting the grease."

When the Sioux commenced to be a problem to the federal government in the 1850's, it responded with attention, gifts, and military force. As a result of difficulties much farther west, General William Harney led an expedition through Sioux country, emerged at the rattletrap Fort Pierre, and quickly decided that a new fort was in order. This new fort was located at a point on the Missouri River called Handy's Point a few miles above the northern limits of Ponca territory. The site was chosen for a number of reasons but prominent among them was the idea that its troops would be in a position to help the Poncas maintain themselves against the Teton Sioux. During the next twenty years, troops from

39

Fort Randall responded on many occasions to the Poncas' need for help. For a while the post established a semi-permanent camp near the Ponca village site at the mouth of the Niobrara. All of this was a stop-gap procedure. It did not really solve the problems for the Poncas, but merely temporarily improved the situation. The Poncas were helped to survive, but not to prosper. They were, in a phrase coined for a different situation, allowed to "twist slowly, slowly in the wind." They were fully aware of their position and did not like it; the raid on the government installations in 1857-58 was a result. The attack did not spring so much from hostility as from frustration.

On March 12, 1858, the Poncas signed a treaty with the federal government that limited the size of their land area and carefully delineated a reservation for them. This reservation included all lands "beginning at a point on the Niobrara River and running N. so as to intersect the Ponca River twenty-five miles from its mouth; thence from said point of intersection up said river twenty miles; then due S. to the Niobrara River; thence down said river to the place of the beginning." This treaty, while setting boundaries, meant that the Poncas were giving up a great deal of territory which they had always claimed and used. In return, the federal government promised to guarantee and protect the tribe's ownership of its newly-defined reservation and to insure the safety of both Ponca persons and of their property.

Shortly after the 1858 treaty went into effect, the

federal government established a separate Ponca Indian Agency on the north side of the mouth of Ponca Creek. This was designed to provide the Poncas with a more responsive bureaucratic brand of service and to show that the federal government was really committed to maintaining these people. Yet, the government came back in 1865 to negotiate another treaty. This one was signed in Washington, D.C.; the government was not taking any chances. The Poncas relinquished approximately 30,000 acres of their reservation. In return, a grateful government "by way of rewarding them for their constant fidelity to the government and citizens thereof, and with a view of returning to the said tribe of Ponca Indians their old burying grounds and corn fields" ceded back these burying grounds and some agricultural lands, as well as the islands in the Niobrara and some land on Ponca Creek. Even then, the United States refused to pay the claims of any settlers living on the land returned to the Poncas. Instead, the tribe was required to pay these squatters out of its own funds. In its usual gracious and generous manner, the government did agree to pay the expenses involved in signing the treaty. The result of all this was that the Poncas retained a reservation of 96,000 acres, more or less, and again had assurances that the Great Father in Washington and his minions in the west would support and protect them. By this time, Poncas must have been more than a little dubious, and subsequent events would wholly confirm their doubts.

During this entire period, the pressure of the Sioux had continued. In 1859, Brule and Oglala Lakota, combined with some Northern Cheyenne, attacked a Ponca hunting camp killing a chief and thirteen others and carrying off three Ponca children into slavery. The Poncas complained bitterly to their agent, and one of the chiefs told that unhappy man that:

> I shall be a woman no longer, but go on the warpath with my tribe as I used to before my Great Father talked softly to me and tied my hands! It is better to die like warriors — like men — not wait until the Sioux come here to kill us.

The next spring the agent requested a small cannon to help the Poncas defend themselves, but its arrival was not much help. That same year the Sioux again spoiled the Ponca hunt, and, when the Poncas attempted to make peace with the Sioux, they were told that they would be left alone for a year, because the Sioux intended to do most of their fighting against the Omahas and the Pawnees.

In 1861, the new agent, J. B. Hoffman, organized a police force from among the warriors of the Ponca tribe. They were fifty men in blue coats and grey pants, who were to secure the Ponca home village, the agency, and the store of supplies. In 1862, a school that stressed the manual arts was also established on the Ponca reservation. This was the first school of this type in the Nebraska-Dakota country. Yet, the Poncas were still not happy with the government. They were not receiving the rifles, the ammunition, and the trade goods that they had been promised. They were experiencing severe difficulties gaining an adequate food supply and maintaining their morale. Things were bad, but they were going to turn much worse.

After the Civil War, the United States finally decided to stop the fight with Red Cloud and the Sioux over the Bozeman Trail to Montana. The result was the Fort Laramie Treaty of 1868. This was the last treaty negotiated with the Sioux and, in some ways, the most famous Indian treaty ever negotiated and signed. By this treaty, the Sioux acquired all of South Dakota west of the Missouri River, as the Great Sioux Reservation, as well as other territory for hunting purposes. The men who signed the treaty did something that to this day is nearly impossible to understand, much less explain. They promised to the Sioux in perpetuity all of the land that the Poncas owned or had owned. The Poncas were in a unique situation, but not a pleasant one. Their treaty of 1858 had guaranteed them their reservation. Yet, the treaty of Fort Laramie gave that land to the Sioux. It also gave the Sioux a perfect excuse to attack the Poncas — not that they needed one. Because of the treaty ratified by the Congress and proclaimed by the President, the Sioux could now legally claim that the Poncas were trespassers and that the Sioux had a perfect right to attack and expel them. The response of government officials to this unheard of situation was typical — they did nothing. They did not attempt to go back to the Sioux and admit that a mistake had been made and attempt to rectify it. They did not even attempt to increase their protection of the Poncas, although such action was clearly in order. They simply went blithely on their way having condemned their friends to a fate that was not yet clear, but that was certain to be unpleasant.

For eight more years this situation continued. The government declined to protect the Ponca people who were their friends and who had never made war upon them. At the same time, the government gave the Teton Sioux large numbers of supplies, including the rifles and ammunition that would be used to kill Poncas.

By the mid-1870's, the government's Indian policy had become totally bankrupt, and the Sioux struck back. Strong elements of all the western Sioux tribes left the reservation because white miners had been allowed to penetrate the Black Hills in 1875 and 1876. These Indians became known as "hostiles." The United States had a full-scale Indian war on its hands — one that reached its high point in the destruction of the immediate command of General George Armstrong Custer on the Little Bighorn River in 1876. At the same time, the Poncas were holding on desperately, trying to survive. In 1876, Congress appropriated $25,000 to remove the Poncas from Nebraska and Dakota to the Indian Territory, present Oklahoma. Eight chiefs were sent to investigate the new reservation and turned in an unfavorable report. Against their wishes, and their best judgment, they were removed anyway — to an area in which they had no desire to settle. Shabby treatment was the norm in most of the relationships of the federal government to the American Indian tribes; but for sheer cowardice and duplicity, nothing can match the treatment afforded the Poncas.

MOVING TO INDIAN TERRITORY

It is usually understood that Indian removal was a United States policy that reached its peak in the 1830's and continued to decline until the time of the American Civil War. This, alas, is untrue. Indian removal ceased to be a stated policy of the United States after 1860 but continued to be practiced until the 1880's. The Poncas were one of the last to be affected by it. While it is possibly true that the government agents who urged Ponca removal had in mind what they considered to be the best interests of the tribe, the Poncas did not agree and were forced to migrate against their will. They were also removed in violation of treaties solemnly agreed to by the United States.

The Poncas, a people of surprising sophistication in the ways of the white man, did not placidly accept removal. They did not fight, because they well knew a war would mean disaster and would destroy them. Instead, they refused to move and hired a lawyer to

45

try to stop the proceedings, paying his fee with thirty head of horses. The lawyer, one man against a powerful government, failed. The United States government sent a wagon train to carry the tribe away and with the train came accompanying soldiers to make certain the trek was completed. The soldiers were not cruel, and indeed, it is said that many of them were very sympathetic to the Poncas, whom they admired. Yet, the move had been ordered and the move would take place.

The tribe was transferred in two parties. The first group consisted of the mixed bloods and was headed by Lone Chief, who was half French. It began its journey to Indian Territory in 1876. The main party consisted mainly of full bloods led by the noted chief, White Eagle. His party left the north in 1879, going south to the Quapaw Indian Reservation immediately south of Baxter Springs, Kansas. The whole experience was hard on the people. Numbers died on the journey. Lone Chief, the leader of the mixed bloods, died at Baxter Springs. All in all, some 800 Poncas finally made it to Indian Territory; a few remained in the north, scattered and confused.

The first area chosen for the Poncas was headquartered at Miami. The Poncas, still a people of the rivers, disliked the area, which they regarded as hot, desolate, and dangerous. Aided by some influential white men, they succeeded in obtaining a new reservation at the eastern edge of the old Cherokee Outlet. Here they stayed, and here their descendants remain to the present time.

The removal of the Poncas to Indian Territory was accomplished by force although no actual hostilities took place. The Poncas did not want to move and it was the presence of the army that forced them to migrate. As a result, there was considerable suffering and hardship. When they reached Baxter Springs, Kansas, the government sent chiefs White Eagle and Standing Bear on an inspection trip to Indian Territory to choose the new reservation. The area involved is around the present-day city of Miami, Oklahoma. The Poncas, under considerable pressure, were forced to accept the land, but they did not like it, and they were determined not to stay there. The agent told them that they were a thousand miles from home, had no money, no interpreter, and no way to survive if they did not do as they were told. Standing Bear accused the agent of stealing the Poncas' money and probably did not improve the tribe's situation by speaking his mind.

The Poncas were very discontented with their original reservation and soon persuaded the government to allow them to select another. The new reservation at the confluence of the Salt Fork and the Arkansas rivers contained 101,894 acres of fertile land. It was more nearly like their homeland in the north than any place the Poncas had yet seen. As a result, they felt a little better when they were once more put in wagons at Baxter Springs. The eight-day march of 185 miles ended on July 29, 1879. Federal

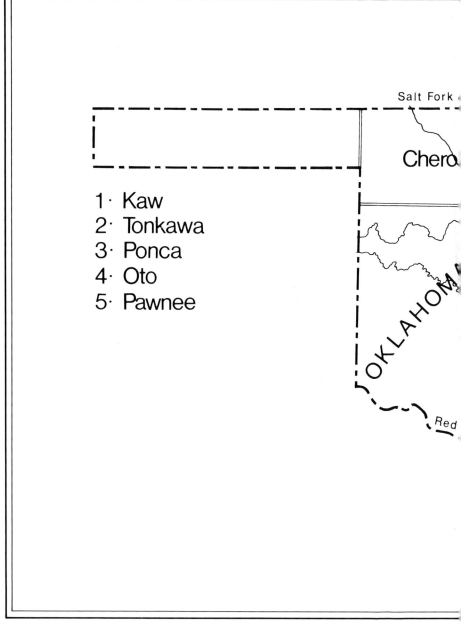

Salt Fork

Chero

1· Kaw
2· Tonkawa
3· Ponca
4· Oto
5· Pawnee

OKLAHOMA

Red

MAP 2. Oklahoma and Certain Indian Territories, 1890-91

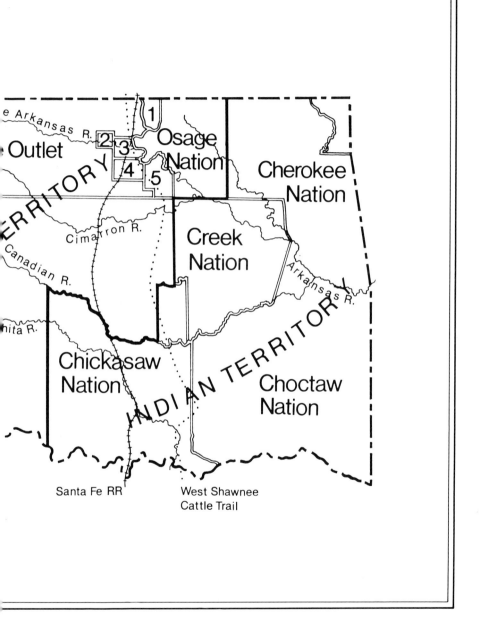

e Arkansas R.

Outlet

1

2 3

4 5

Osage Nation

Cherokee Nation

Cimarron R.

Canadian R.

Creek Nation

Arkansas R.

hita R.

Chickasaw Nation

INDIAN TERRITORY

Choctaw Nation

Santa Fe RR

West Shawnee Cattle Trail

officials did make efforts to please the Poncas. They began immediately to erect office buildings, shops, and schools. The school was named in honor of White Eagle, who was the paramount chief. Some of the people preferred to live in tipis, while others built log houses according to their individual preferences. Plows and planting tools were provided, and it was hoped that even though summer was waning, some sort of a crop could be raised before winter. During 1879, still more improvements were made on the reservation. An industrial building was erected so that farm equipment could be repaired. A large boarding school was put up to accommodate children living too far away to commute. All of this is not to suggest, however, that life for the Poncas was idyllic. A number of people died during the winter and in the ensuing spring. The change in water and climate had taken its toll. Although the government provided a beef ration, food was in short supply and housing conditions were very bad. All this coming after a severe winter caused much unrest among the Indians, and they began to hold councils to decide what to do about their future. At one such council meeting, Standing Bear spoke eloquently about his desire to return to his homeland. Although he had been one of the men who had made the Indian Territory inspection trip, he had opposed transfer from Nebraska at every occasion. He spoke with great conviction to his fellows, arguing that the Poncas could no longer live in the country they now

51

inhabited and that they must return to the north to avoid extinction. White Eagle opposed him. Although he did not like the move himself, he felt the tribe had no real choice and that the government was trying its best to help. He further emphasized that the Poncas had not been there long enough to really test the terrain. As a result of all the oratory, the majority of the Poncas agreed to remain in Oklahoma, rather than running the risks inherent in leaving against the wishes of the government.

Standing Bear, however, would not relent. His son had been one of those who died during that first winter. According to the father, his dying words had been a request to take his body back to his homeland in Nebraska to be buried with those of his ancestors. A broken-hearted father, along with thirty members of the tribe, placed the remains of the dead boy in a wagon and set out for their old home in the Niobrara of the north. They traveled three months, and finally in the spring they reached the Omaha Reservation along the Missouri south of the Niobrara. They had no home of their own in the north. Their land was gone and another tribe occupied it; but the Omahas took pity upon them and gave them land to farm and furnished them seed to put in the ground. They adjusted quickly and peacefully and were well satisfied and contented until the soldiers from Fort Randall appeared. The soldiers arrested Standing Bear after he refused to return to the Indian Territory. He and all thirty of his fellow tribesmen were imprisoned at Fort Omaha and charged with willfully leaving the reservation where the government had placed them without their permission.

The United States goverment at that time believed that Indians on reservations were under its total control, and that the government had a perfect right to select those reservations and confine the Indians there. The attempt of the government to practice this policy had triggered the attack on Custer and the annihilation of his command in 1876. Apparently the bureaucrats had learned nothing from this disaster. Official policy required any Indian who left a reservation to have a pass signed by his agent. If he lacked this written permission, he could be — and indeed often was — locked up and otherwise punished at the whim of the benevolent federal government. This was a power that the government and its Indian Service had assumed without either legislative or judicial authority. They exercised it everywhere, and it went unchallenged. Now, however, the courts were at last about to take a good long look at the government's position.

When Standing Bear and his thirty fellow tribesmen were unceremoniously tossed in jail and charged with escaping the reservation, the government confiscated all their property and ordered the Omahas to deny them shelter. United States officials went further, and paid annuities required by treaty to the portion of the tribe that remained on its reservation in Indian Territory, but paid nothing to those who had journeyed north. In order fully to define its intentions, the Bureau of Indian Affairs issued an order expressly forbidding those Poncas who chose to leave Indian Territory from taking any property with them whatsoever under penalty of being arrested for theft. As it was impossible for anyone to travel any distance without supplies, the edict, in effect, made the Poncas prisoners on their reservation for as long as the government thought it necessary or desirable. Uncle Sam had cracked down, and, after all, what could thirty-one jailed and impoverished Poncas do? As it turned out, they could do plenty, and they would receive much help in the doing.

The plight of the Poncas attracted attention first in Omaha and then nationwide. The editor of the *Omaha Herald,* Dr. George L. Miller, took up their cause and broadcast their predicament to the nation and indeed to the world. Two attorneys, A. J. Poppleton and John L. Webster, became interested in the case, both from a humanitarian viewpoint and from a desire to test the legal questions involved. The major point in question was whether the federal government had the legal right to imprison an Indian who had committed no crime. The lawyers secured a writ of habeas corpus and the prisoner, Standing Bear, was duly delivered to the district court of the United States at Omaha where these issues would be heard. Reporters arrived from all over the country and watched as the Honorable G. M. Lamberton, the attorney for the government, argued that an Indian was not entitled to the right of habeas corpus because he was not "a citizen or person under the law." The lawyers defending Standing Bear first raised the question that if an Indian was not a person, then what was he? If he was a person, certainly the protection of habeas corpus, as well as other constitutional guarantees, must be his or American freedom would be meaningless. As it turned out, the best argument for Standing Bear was the man himself. He spoke through an interpreter and, even with such an awkward device, his words came through with eloquence and his points were well made:

> There is one God and he hath made Indian and white man. We are all made of the same dust of the earth. He made me red and you white, and although we are of different colors our hearts are all the same. I have committed no crime except I am an Indian.

Because the trial revolved around a point of law, there was no jury. Judge Elmer Dundee, after a hearing of several days, ruled that Standing Bear and his fellow tribesmen were being held unlawfully and that they must be released from custody. Standing Bear, after the judge's ruling had been interpreted to him, spoke once again. He thanked the judge and praised him for his sense of justice, and he thanked his lawyers, saying that "before when we were wronged we Indians went on the warpath against the white man. We had no law to punish those who did wrong but you have found a much better way. Now I have no more use for a tomahawk." He then walked to the front of the judge's bench, placed his tomahawk on the floor, stood with his arms crossed and said, "I have found a better way." He then picked up the tomahawk and handed it to his attorney, John Webster, and told him, "This is the only way I can pay you. Keep it as a remembrance, a memorial of a great victory you have gained. I have now no use for it; I will follow the ways of peace." Standing Bear then led his small band to the Omaha reservation to make a home, to farm, and to become what is now known as the Northern Ponca tribe.

The plight of the Poncas and the courageous struggle waged by Standing Bear caused the Commissioner of Indian Affairs to rethink the policy of moving northern Indians into the southern plains. He concluded that the whole thing had been a mistake, and that the radical change of climate, different farming conditions, and the high death rate made such transfers undesirable. Yet, the majority of Ponca was forced to remain in the south, if for no other reason than because their land in the north was gone.

The opinion of Judge Dundee would be appealed all the way to the Supreme Court. His major contention was:

> . . . that an Indian is a person within the law of the United States and has, therefore, the right to sue out of writ of habeas corpus where he is restrained of liberty in violation of the Constitution or laws, and that the Indian has an inalienable right to life, liberty and the pursuit of happiness as long as he obeys the laws and does not trespass on forbidden ground.

BIG SMOKE, A PONCA WARRIOR, holding a tomahawk, probably one of the same type that Chief Standing Bear presented to his attorney after a federal district court freed him from army detention.

This point went far beyond its effect on Standing Bear and his small group and was ultimately applied to all American Indians. It seems a striking injustice that an Indian in North America would have to prove to anyone that he is a person. Yet, this was the case, and Standing Bear was the man who did it.

Standing Bear next attempted to have his people restored to their old landholdings. The government did not do so because it claimed that it could not. The land in question belonged to the Sioux, according to the United States government. Standing Bear and his people eventually settled on an island which had been part of the old Ponca reservation, and which had been overlooked in the sale of the land to the Sioux. In the meantime, his case went through the appeal process, first to the United States circuit court and finally to Justice Samuel Miller of the Supreme Court of the United States. On June 5, 1880, the appeal was dismissed on motion of the United States District Attorney, and the Poncas were home free.

In April of 1880, the Poncas sued Red Cloud, as leader of the Sioux, and in May of the same year the Ponca tribe also sued the Sioux tribe in an attempt to recover their territory and to establish title to as much of the old reservation as there was in the state of Nebraska. On August 11, 1881, the Sioux agreed to give the Poncas land, and peace was made between the two tribes. The Sioux did not relinquish all the land taken from the Poncas, but it represented a considerable portion. In 1881, President Rutherford

B. Hayes appointed a commission to inquire into the matter of the lost Ponca land, and the Senate also appointed a committee to investigate the same matter. The government by then had reversed its position and had taken the attitude that the Poncas were really better off in Indian Territory. Standing Bear and White Eagle appeared before Congress, and a bill was introduced in both the House and the Senate to restore their lands on the old reservation and to put their homes and farms back in the same condition they had been prior to removal. The Senate committee investigating the matter stated that "the Poncas have been forced without authority or law" from their homes to the Indian Territory and reported that they favored a bill to restore them to their former homes and appropriated $50,000 for the purpose of taking them back and "to restore their dilapidated homes." The same report charged the government with violating the rights of "a people who were friendly, peaceable, and orderly."

Secretary of the Interior Carl Schurz was not at all certain that the Poncas had any right to sue the United States government or any state. He felt, as was true of most "reformers" in that period, that it was necessary for all Indians to transform themselves from a tribal to an individual lifestyle as well as to change their property from communal to individual ownership. In this he was anticipating the Dawes Severalty Act, which would be passed in 1887. The whole idea of this policy was that the Indian should be assimilated into white society in order to gain the protection of its laws for themselves and their property. Schurz was entirely sincere and well-meaning in this. He believed as long as a tribe held a large reservation with a considerable portion of unused land, at least unused in the white sense of the term, that they would be a people with no fixed homes. As an American Victorian, Schurz thought that a fixed home was terribly important and was something that the American Indian would or should welcome. The gift of individual land ownership, combined with a strong educational policy, was his solution to the "Indian problem."

The Senate committee investigating the Ponca situation decided that the Indians in the north should be allowed to remain and allotted some 26,236 acres in Knox County, Nebraska to the 136 people led by Standing Bear. The same committee also stated that the Poncas who remained in Oklahoma had received better land than those who had returned to the north and that full payment had been made to all those who had lost property because of the removal.

Standing Bear himself continued to live in the north and to be a figure of both respect and power among the Poncas and among the white community. He lived a long life and died at his home in Niobrara, Nebraska on September 3, 1908. A great man, he had fought for his tribe's rights and the rights of all American Indians to be considered people under the law. It was a fight that he had won, and countless generations were to be in his debt.

60

When the Poncas received their final reservation in Oklahoma on the eastern edge of the Cherokee Outlet, they had a total of just over 101,000 acres of land. The land was fertile and well watered. At the same time they received the reservation, they came into contact with a new group of white men, some who were friends and some who were not. Prominent among the latter were the Millers — Colonel George W. Miller and his sons, George, Joseph, and Zach. Their influence on the Poncas would be long lasting and, in the long run, disastrous.

To be fair to the Millers, they were not consciously hostile to the Poncas, nor did they desire to harm them. It is simply a case of a family that had an overwhelming ambition to advance its own interests, and woe to anyone who happened to be in the way. The Poncas had earlier been in the way of the Teton Sioux, and they lost their land. Now they were in the way of the Millers, and they lost their land again. This time it was lost without bloodshed, which was, perhaps, an improvement.

Colonel George Miller was a former Confederate who had sold out his interests in the South and started for California in 1870. He stopped in Missouri and became a cattle driver to the railhead at Baxter Springs, Kansas. He found this business profitable and, looking at the country, decided that he would establish himself in the cattle business. Southerners of the planter class tended to think big, and, while the old plantation run by slave labor was no longer a possibility, enormous baronies of range land supporting vast herds of cattle were not only possible, but the coming thing. The Colonel started his cattle business on the Quapaw Indian Reservation near Miami, Indian Territory. He was there when the federal government moved the Poncas into that area from their homeland in Nebraska. The Poncas were, as has been stated, most unhappy in the Quapaw country, and Colonel Miller came to their aid. He helped them persuade the government to move them to a new location in what would become Kay and Noble counties in the old Cherokee Outlet. Miller leased some 60,000 acres from the Cherokees in 1879 and, in the following year, moved his base of operations to Baxter Springs, Kansas where his youngest son, George, was born. He bought out his partner the same year and abandoned his old brand, "K", for the new brand "101" which, by sheer lack of coincidence, corresponded exactly with the number of acres in the Ponca reservation. "101" was a brand, an acreage, and for a time, perhaps the most famous of the western cattle ranches.

In 1892, the Millers moved their headquarters and their cattle down the Salt Fork to the Ponca Indian reservation. The Poncas were still extremely friendly to Colonel Miller, who had helped them obtain the reservation, and they offered the Millers their entire reservation on lease for the purpose of grazing cattle. The lease was duly signed, and the ranch established in a dugout in a bluff on the south bank of the Salt Fork. The family continued to live in Kansas, because it was still not possible to build permanent headquarters on the reservation until the Dawes Act of 1887 was applied to the Poncas. This act allotted land to the Indians on an individual basis, encouraged them to farm it, and to acquire individual titles over a period of time. The surplus land, that is, the land that would be above and beyond what the Indians were individually allotted, would be available for sale. When this happened, the Millers would be ready to move, though it did not occur until 1903 — the year the old Colonel died on his ranch. The Miller brothers decided to run the ranch as a partnership. They made a great deal of money and plowed it back into buying land from the Poncas at what appear to have been very low prices. Although they never succeeded in buying the whole reservation, they came fairly close. In any event, the combination of their purchases and leases meant that the Miller brothers continued to dominate the reservation economically for as long as the ranch remained in operation.

As time passed, and the Millers became less dependent on Ponca good will, their arrogance increased. They fenced extensively and removed Poncas who dared to "trespass" on their own reservation. There were rumors that some Poncas had been shot for entering the sacred confines of the ranch. In any event, it was certain that anyone coming to the ranch without permission would soon be confronted with armed riders who would assist him, gently or other-

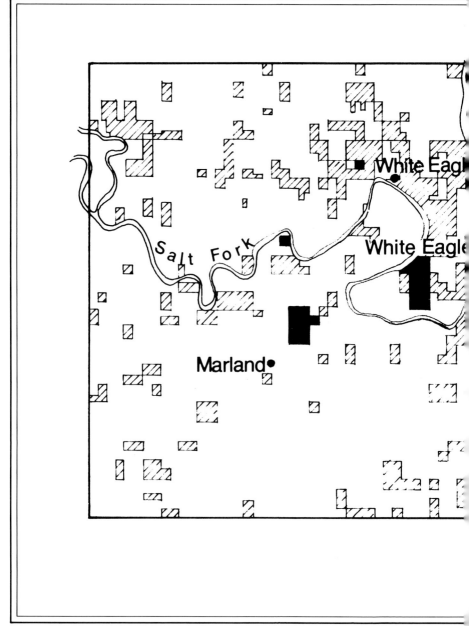

Salt Fork

White Eag[le]

White Eagl[e]

Marland●

MAP 3. Individual and Tribal Land Holdings on the Ponca Reservation, 1975.

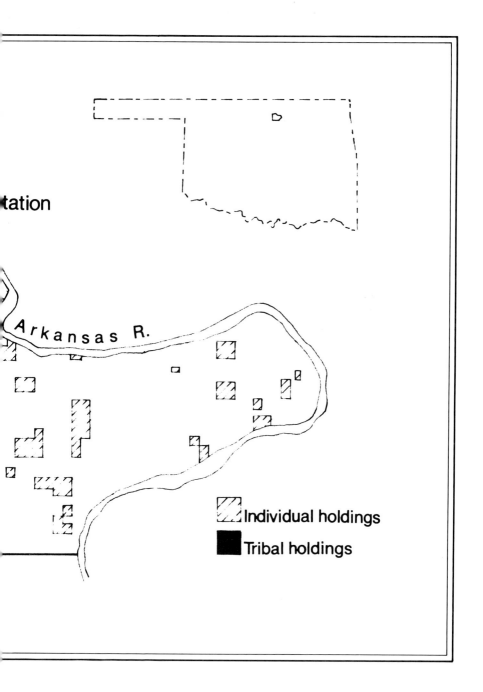

tation

Arkansas R.

Individual holdings

Tribal holdings

wise, to leave the premises in the fastest possible manner.

The owners of the 101 Ranch did many things other than raise cattle. For one thing, they put on wild west shows and rodeos for fun and profit. Their big show was touring Europe when World War I broke out, and, by that time, they were famous throughout the world. They also got into the oil business. By opening up the Ponca reservation to partnership and lease arrangements, they released great sources of oil and money. The three brothers combined their talents: Joe was the agriculturalist; Zach was the horse and cattleman; and George was the modern businessman. The ranch continued to expand. It processed its own agricultural produce, it had its own packing plant, its own dairy, its own poultry operation. It also had a tannery, a leather and harness factory, a fruit cannery, a creamery, an oil refinery, a cider mill, a machine shop, a blacksmith shop, an ice plant, a filling station, and a power plant. The Millers even produced motion pictures. In 1923, the income of the ranch from oil alone was over $1,300,000. The ranch by then was out of debt, and the land expansion period over.

In the 1920's, however, things started to go sour for the 101. In 1927, Joseph Miller was killed. Severe drought and crop failures, even floods, ate away at the profits of the ranch. In 1929, George Miller was killed in an automobile accident. At the same time, a surplus of oil developed in the United States, and revenues from this source were drastically reduced. The Panic of 1929 finally brought the Millers' unwieldly operation to an end. More loans were taken out, but as prices fell and taxes continued, the ranch plunged into a financial abyss, and in 1931, a receiver was appointed and liquidation begun.

Regardless of the outcome of the Millers' adventures, it is apparent that they opened up vast sources of wealth and huge amounts of money were made. It is also apparent that the Poncas and their lands were the basis of all this wealth and that these Indians gained very little from it. It was never a case of sheer illegality, but rather of sharp, hard-driving business practices, which ran rampant over the Poncas, because they did not as yet have sufficient sophistication to handle them. The Poncas were not crippled as much by the Millers as by the Sioux, but the results were similar. Out of the 101,000 acres that once comprised the Ponca reservation, there are today 9,185 acres in Kay County and 8,247 in Noble County that are Indian owned. The Ponca tribe, as an entity, owns exactly 785 acres of land. This is a tragedy; it is something that should never have been allowed to occur by a government that had charge of that land as the trustee of the Ponca people.

THE HOTTEST BRAND GOING

Not all white men who associated with the Poncas were unkind, rapacious, or cruel. There was another type — the true philanthropist. One of the great examples of this type was E. W. Marland, a man who combined high business success and acumen with philanthropic virtues. Marland was the long-time and devoted friend of White Eagle and many of the other Poncas. He was a most unusual fellow. Born to an English father, who had married an older American woman, Marland grew from a prissy little boy, on whom the other children picked, to become a multi-millionaire, a connoisseur of the arts, a friend of the Indian, and governor of Oklahoma. He died broke, but he lived well, and, in some ways, he lived nobly.

Marland's father made a great deal of money in the Pittsburgh area. E. W. himself achieved some success in the oil and gas business in Pennsylvania before heading west. By the time he became involved with the Miller brothers and the 101 Ranch, he was pretty much on his uppers and had to borrow large sums in order to wildcat on the Ponca reservation. He and George Miller organized the 101 Ranch Oil Company and drilled the first oil well on the Ponca reserve. This company would expand very rapidly as more and more oil was struck and as production increased. Marland reorganized it as the Marland Refining Company and then as the Marland Oil Company. He designed the familiar triangle-shaped emblem, and it nearly destroyed him when the Continental Oil Company absorbed his operation, and Marland's name was replaced on that triangle with the word "Conoco."

Marland built Ponca City from a scraggly, dusty plains town into the lovely small city that it is today.

69

His first house, which is today a museum, was an edifice of taste and beauty, and he had five blocks of formal gardens, as well as his own golf course. Harking back to his British antecedents, he also organized fox hunting on the Ponca reservation. Marland, his family, and his friends rode to the hounds across the rugged Oklahoma landscape. The foxes, alas, had to be imported. The first one to be released became so frightened of the coyotes that he jumped back in the car that had taken him out to the hunting fields. Such occurrences did not prevent Marland from continuing his sport over the years, and one wonders what the reaction of the Poncas must have been to men and women mounted on hunters and shouting cries like "Yoicks" while galloping madly across the reservation. The Poncas, however, were a long-suffering and tolerant people with a good sense of humor, and they undoubtedly enjoyed the show.

The Poncas also enjoyed E. W. Marland, who helped them in many ways. He gave them money, helped send their children to school, served as their advocate in the state and in Washington, and provided many of them with health care. Beyond that, he gave them that rarest of all commodities — respect. Marland never looked down on the Ponca people, nor did he regard them as his inferiors. It was not at all unusual to see a Ponca Indian in tribal regalia in the midst of a Marland party, which might, at the same time, include men and women of

LITTLE HOLE, AN OKLAHOMA PONCA, wearing long braids and ornate costume such as might be seen at a Marland social gathering.

the higher levels of society dressed in formal attire. The respect given by Marland was returned by the Poncas. Throughout his whole career, they genuinely liked him, and he liked them. They supported him; he supported them. When his companies came to disaster in the late 1920's and early 1930's, and his money vanished, they remained his friends, and the respect was still there. He is still honored in their memories as few white men ever are.

THE DESTRUCTION OF A RESERVATION

The Ponca reservation in Oklahoma provided good farm land, oil, and considerable grazing potential. A people as industrious as the Poncas probably could have made it a prosperous homeland had they been allowed to do so. The policy of leasing the entire reservation to the Miller brothers' ranch proved to be nothing short of a disaster. The oil development, while it did not directly injure the Poncas, also did not help them much. A few fortunate people made some money from the oil leases, but the great majority received nothing. Even so, the thing that injured them most was the allotment of the reservation under the Dawes Act of 1887. The Poncas had, in 1890 and 1893, refused to sell their reservation, but they did allow the workings of this act to continue, and, as a result, the land moved into the hands of individuals and the surplus was sold. The reservation became Kay and Noble counties in the state of Oklahoma as the Poncas lost most of their land base.

Economic loss is a horrible thing. It saps the

morale and shakes the faith of people in the future. It can be overcome by other things; religion, education, and a clinging to the old traditions can help a people to survive poverty and its results. These, too, failed the Poncas. When the land went, much went with it. The move to Oklahoma itself had cut many of their tangible ties with the past. The old landmarks, the burying grounds, the sacred sites were all hundreds of miles away. They became a displaced people without roots. As a result, they tended to lose many of the things that had tied them together. Their religion, in the old sense, slowly drifted away and fell into disuse. The Christians moved in to try to replace it. A Methodist mission was established on the reservation as early as 1890, while Baptists and others also picked up many adherents. Yet, it takes much time to replace a religion that permeates all phases of a people's life, and even the entry of peyote and the Native American Church could not replace all that had been lost.

Education also failed the people. Their own system of education, which had involved the systematic training of the young to fit their lifestyle by the Missouri River, no longer seemed to apply. Although a boarding school was opened in 1883 and other schools followed, the type of education that was introduced succeeded mainly in breaking down the old culture without replacing it with a new and better one. Ponca children were taught to reject their own heritage and language and to adopt those of the Americans. Such things are not done quickly and for decades many people were in a void — almost a vacuum — between one culture and another.

The health of the people also suffered in Oklahoma. The Poncas were northerners used to crisp air and cold winters. Now they were in the south, where there was malaria and other fevers, which their bodies could not resist. Weakened by the removal, ill-fed and unhappy in their new location, the Poncas watched their death rate rise. Infant mortality was high, and tuberculosis, the white death, stalked tribal members. The hospitalization and medical care provided by the federal government proved helpful, but was inadequate.

By the 1920's, the Poncas were in deep peril as were most American Indians. The so-called Merriam Report, issued by the Brookings Institute in 1928, made public the terrible conditions under which the Indians of the United States were living and shocked the government into moving toward massive policy changes. Among the first things done was the de facto cessation of the sale of individual allotments during the Hoover administration. This policy became law in 1934 after Franklin D. Roosevelt brought his New Deal into power. Steps were taken to increase congressional appropriations for Indian education and health care. It was again, however, a case of too little and too late, but it was a start in the right direction.

When Roosevelt took office in 1933 and appointed John Collier as Indian Commissioner, the "New Deal" for the American Indian began. Collier's great contribution was the passage and the implementation of the Indian Reorganization Act, which provided for the institution of elective self-government among the tribes that voted to accept it. This Indian Reorganization Act, however, did not apply to the Indians of Oklahoma. By the 1930's, they had been so stricken by land loss that, with the exception of the Osages, they no longer had anything that the federal government would or could recognize as reservations. Put another way, there were no longer the contiguous blocs of land inhabited and owned by tribes and individuals in sufficient volume to warrant calling them reservations. The Oklahoma Indians could not even qualify as "open reservations" as could many of the more heavily penetrated reserves in the north. They were indeed in dire straits, for the New Deal did not apply to them.

The result was that two years after the passage of the Indian Reorganization Act, Congress passed a special law allowing Oklahoma Indians to organize. This was the Oklahoma Indian Welfare Act of June 26, 1936. In time, the Poncas organized under it and reestablished a tribal government, which was elective and not based upon hereditary chieftainships. Its passage coincided closely with the death of the last of the tribe's hereditary chiefs, Horse Chief Eagle, who died in 1940.

The constitution and by-laws of the Poncas, as finally amended and refurbished in 1950, provided for a governing body of seven elected members. This governing body was dubbed the business committee

75

and each man served a two-year term. This committee, in turn, selected the tribal chairman. A tribal roll was also established: an individual was required to have at least one-fourth Ponca Indian blood to gain full membership in the tribe. Likewise, provisions were made for regular elections and meetings of the business committee, and the tribe passed a bill of rights and by-laws, which established rules for conducting business. All of this was duly approved by the Secretary of the Interior, and the Poncas then had a new type of government with which to attempt to revive and sustain themselves as a tribe.

New Deal relief programs assisted many of the Poncas during the 1930's. The WPA, NYA, CCC, and many others provided employment and brought money to tribal members. As the Depression ended, many young Ponca men went off to war as they had in 1917. The net result was that during and after World War II, more and more Poncas left what land remained and moved to towns and cities on or near the reservations in order to find employment. Some continued to farm, many worked in the oil refineries, some worked in construction, some in retail businesses. Most, however, continued to struggle through life and to feel that, even in towns on their old reservation, that there was great prejudice against them. The prejudice was frequently clandestine and subtle. Few Poncas could be found working in the better business establishments in Ponca City or other such towns; the better jobs went to others.

At the same time, education was improving. The

Ponca children for the most part, attended integrated schools, and the improvements in instruction were considerable. Even so, much was left to be desired. The number of students who went on to higher education was very small, and, of those who succeeded, few returned to help their people.

Culturally, the Poncas tried to retain what was left of the old traditions and the old ways. The Ponca business committee assumed the sponsorship of the annual summer powwow that had been held annually since 1881. Parents tried to teach the language, although in a tribe that was becoming increasingly mixed in its background, this became very difficult. The old religion was lost. Many of the arts, crafts, games, and the like also disappeared — perhaps forever. The one thing that was revived was a degree of hope, and this was important. The Poncas could move into the modern era with at least some faith that things might improve in the future for themselves and for their children.

THE NATIVE AMERICAN CHURCH AND PEYOTE

Today, the Poncas have lost or rejected nearly all the remnants of their early native religion. The great majority of them belongs to various Christian denominations. The Poncas are an intensely religious people; they are devout in their attendance. The only Native American religious gathering that remains to them is that of the peyote ritual.

Peyote is the dried form of a cactus that grows in northern Mexico and along the Texas border country. It is regarded as being hallucinogenic by the doctors and other specialists who have studied it. It is non-addicting, and no one has, as yet, proven that there are any permanent harmful effects from using it. Its users among the Indians reject the conclusion that it is a hallucinogenic and regard it as having "power." This power, religious in nature, is said to release the inner being of the user and allow him to approach the natural and supernatural world with enhanced understanding and sensitivity.

The peyote ritual was not native to the Poncas in Nebraska, nor did they adopt it as soon as they went to Indian Territory, because peyote is not indigenous to that region either. The use of peyote came from the south and was brought to the Indian Territory by southern tribes. According to one noted authority, the Southern Ponca received it from the Cheyenne in 1902. Some present-day Poncas assert that they received it from the Tonkawas, who were removed from Texas to Oklahoma in the late 1860's and have used peyote down to the present time. It is certain that the Ponca and the Tonkawa ceremonies are very similar.

The Ponca ceremony is performed in a tipi, or, nowadays, in a house, and it is always held at night. When all the people are assembled, the leader first prays, and then all the members pray while smoking prayer cigarettes. The peyote is then distributed in the form of dried "buttons," which are eaten. This corresponds very closely to the sacrament of the Last Supper in the Christian religion. After eating the peyote button, singing begins. Each person sings four songs to the accompaniment of a gourd rattle which he shakes, and a drum made of brass and partially filled with water, which is played by the man on his right. The pitch of the drum can be changed by tilting it, and allowing the water to hit the drum head.

The ceremony, which starts around eight o'clock in the evening, continues for many hours. At midnight, there are more prayers by the leaders, and the people drink water as a ritual. They continue to sing and pray all night. When dawn breaks, breakfast becomes a ceremony, and everyone eats corn, fruit, and other native foods. The leader then closes the meeting by singing four songs.

The peyote religion, or cult as some call it, that came up from the south was organized on an informal basis. One of the major problems was that the peyote itself was very difficult to obtain. Both the federal and state governments regarded it as a narcotic and tried to stamp out its sale, transportation, and use. At the same time, the Christian denominations adamantly opposed it, because it seemed to them that it posed an alternative to Christianity, even though its users did not regard it as such. Even today, the Ponca see no reason why one cannot practice the peyote religion and, at the same time, be a good practicing Christian. In the early days, however, all this opposition made the use of peyote very difficult. In the period beginning in 1914, the people who used peyote began to charter the Native American

CHIEFS OF THE PONCA NATION with a United States Indian Agent, the local representative

of a capricious national government intolerant of traditional tribal leaders.

Church under the laws of the particular states where they lived. They formed their church to achieve legality and to make viable their argument that preventing the transportation of peyote was interfering with their religious practices, and thus violated the Constitution of the United States. For a long time, this argument did not gain acceptance, but since the 1960's it seems to be prevailing.

The Ponca of today see no evil in their use of peyote. Not all use it, but probably a majority does. Users regard it as a help, rather than as a hindrance, and feel that its effects are beneficial. They combine the use of peyote in their ceremonies with considerable Christianity. The New Testament is commonly found on their altars, and prayers are offered to Jesus Christ, among others. The Poncas regard anyone who interferes with the peyote ceremony as a person who is robbing them of their right to religious freedom, and who is to argue with them?

THE PRESENT

In 1950, the Poncas adopted a new constitution, but it did not significantly alter their form of government. The tribal business committee of seven members continued to be the legislative branch of the government, and it elected one of its members to be the chief executive. Because they were not recognized as having a true reservation, either open or closed, the Poncas did not establish a judicial system to handle the lower levels of law and order, domestic relations, and the like. In a situation where the land

82

base was small and the tribal membership was scattered and living primarily in towns, there seemed to be no real need for a court system; and this has proven, for the most part, to be true.

As time went on, and the pressures of more and more federal programs, as well as demands from the Indian people themselves increased, the Poncas developed more extended inter-tribal relationships. They became part of the North Central Inter-tribal Council, which was composed of the Poncas and the four tribes represented by the agency at Pawnee, Oklahoma. In addition, they joined the twenty-three tribes of western Oklahoma in an organization that would attempt to bring the combined pressure of these tribes to bear upon the state, the Bureau of Indian Affairs, and the federal government in general. These organizations, while proving cumbersome at times, are useful. Small tribes on unrecognized reservations frequently lack the clout necessary to make their wishes known and to get their programs accepted. These organizations gave those Indians an added influence that was helpful, but working within them proved difficult. With a tribal office at White Eagle, an agency office at Pawnee sixty miles away, and an area office of the BIA at Anadarko, well over 150 miles away, Ponca problems of coordination and arranging meetings prove extremely difficult. Yet, dedicated men with an urgent desire to help their people usually find ways. They also find ways, and means, to make the frequent trips to Washington that become increasingly necessary as tribes are forced to deal, not only with the BIA, but also with a plethora of federal agencies that directly, or indirectly, affect their lives and futures.

In the 1950's, the Poncas managed to escape the federal drive to terminate their tribe. Termination, which was a congressional policy designed to break all ties between the federal government and the Indian tribes and to bring the Indian people into the "mainstream" of American society, brought enormous pressures to bear on tribes like the Ponca. The Poncas, who were a traditional people who had also learned to function well in American society, were particularly susceptible to the covetous eyes cast upon them by the congressional terminators. Yet, they resisted and resisted successfully.

In addition, they were relatively unaffected by the federal relocation policies of the same period. These policies were designed to remove Indians from the reservation into major cities, where they would presumably be given some slight training, find jobs and housing, and become self-supporting. The program was designed to remove Indians from the budget of the federal government. This was how the Congress viewed it, but the Indians viewed it quite differently. They regarded it as an attempt by the federal government to dodge responsibilities, which were not only moral obligations but sometimes actually legal ones. The Poncas have accomplished considerable relocation on their own. Many Ponca men and women had already left their homeland in World War II to work in labor-short war industries, and they never returned. Still others found employment in off-reservation cities such as Wichita, Kansas, and Oklahoma City. They had, it is true, made themselves successful and self-supporting, but they did not agree that their independence relieved the federal government of all obligations to either themselves or to their tribe.

In the movements off the reservation and off the land, the Poncas experienced certain amounts of what they felt to be prejudice. This prejudice was not written into law, nor was it overt. Rather, it was subtle and economic in nature. In Oklahoma, politicians bragged about having Indian ancestors or even wives, but many people disliked competing on an equal basis with the Poncas in the economic job market. Thus it is that in a place like Ponca City, which was built with money extracted from the Ponca reservation and its people. Poncas hold jobs at the lower end of the economic ladder. The Poncas would be the first to admit that this is not the result of any organized or concerted plan or plot. It just seems to happen that way. This is, nevertheless, a cause for concern and anger that proves to be especially bitter among the young people who are seeking a better life. Perhaps time will solve this problem if people try to help time along.

The loss of Ponca land is of grave concern to the people. Well over four-fifths of the reservation is gone, and much that remains is of little use to its owners. The individual Ponca who owns an allotment frequently does not farm it, although the

85

Ponca reservation has some of the richest wheatland in the entire world. The land is frequently, and indeed usually, leased to large-scale operators who have sufficient capital to farm on a large scale with expensive mechanized equipment. The Ponca receives lease money, but even if it is a fair price for the lease, the leasee — by the very nature of things — would not be leasing it if he did not expect to make a great deal of money. Thus the full potential for income is not being realized from Ponca land by the Ponca people. To change this system would require intensive land buying programs and the consolidation of Ponca land into large enough units to be commercially feasible. There is no money for this as yet, and even worse, there are no prospects.

Much of the remaining Ponca land is tied up with the problems of heirship. The BIA originally allotted land to an individual. If he or she did not sell, and if he or she did not make a will designating a single heir, that land would be divided among an allottee's heirs-at-law in the following generation. This process continued through several generations. As a result, today, a single quarter section of land may very well have eighty to 100 owners, each with an undivided interest. The land obviously could not be used by all of them, so leasing became the only way to obtain any production and any income. Yet, individual checks for one person's annual undivided interest in a quarter section of land have been issued in amounts as small as one cent. This problem is not helped by time. Time makes it worse, as succeeding generations can only bring more and more heirs. The answer, again, lies in the hope that sufficient capital will appear to buy out all interests and consolidate the land under either individual or tribal ownership. The capital to accomplish this is simply not available, and a lack of land continues and hampers the efforts of the Ponca people to better themselves.

One area where the Poncas have made considerable progress and expect to make more is in the field of housing. For a long time their housing was very substandard and some of it continues to be. Yet, since the mid 1960's, considerable progress has been made. Over 100 separate dwellings have been built, most of them in the area of White Eagle where the tribal offices are located. Prospects for more housing are good, and better housing means higher morale and better health for the people. The Poncas acquired decent housing later than many tribes because the government was reluctant to recognize their reservation. They have managed to work around that attitude in the field of housing and hope to do it in many other areas as well.

The Poncas are very adaptable people. Their old clans are still active, although altered. The Osage clan, for example, which tends to be made up of people who intermarried with the Osages, functions more as a club. Other clans have done the same thing, so there is an Inter-tribal Club, a Victory Club, and the Gives Water Club. In addition, the Ponca tribe has its own American Legion Post No. 38, and it is a very popular gathering place. The

Poncas went to war in both world wars, and the young men usually volunteered for service. As a result, the people have always been proud of their soldiers and still are.

In recent years, the Poncas have been taking increasing advantage of programs being made available to them. They are, for example, involved in the National Congress of American Indians and other organizations. They have developed an Indian Action Program that gives vocational training to adults in heavy equipment operation, carpentry, painting, automobile mechanics, and other similar areas. In addition, they are also involved in the Oklahoma Native American Program, various youth programs, and the Comprehensive Training Act, which gave the Poncas $105,000. In addition, they have established a state-run vocational-technical school in Ponca City where many young Poncas go to be trained. They have also received over $3 million from a claim involving the northern lands that were lost during removal. This money was partially distributed on a per capita basis and partially invested to benefit the tribe as a whole.

It can be readily seen that the Poncas are moving ahead rather rapidly. They do have problems that Indian tribes with more formally recognized reservations do not have, but they are starting to find ways to solve them. Their assets do not, at first glance, appear to be large, but they have one advantage, which is always with them and which is highly significant. This asset is the people themselves, and it is an asset that few can match and none surpass.

THE NORTHERN PONCA

When Standing Bear finally achieved his right to stay in the north, he and his followers settled for a time on an island in the Niobrara River that had been part of the old reservation. Other Poncas who had come back from Indian Territory joined him, and together they tried to reestablish their old way of life. This was not entirely possible, for they no longer had a large reservation in the north with a sufficient land base to support the old lifestyle. The Northern Poncas were no longer able to cultivate their old fields, and the buffalo hunting days were completely behind them. Thus, they held on as well as possible — farming as best they could, hunting a little, and receiving a minimum of help from the government.

In time, these Northern Poncas were given individual land allotments in their old territory in northeastern Nebraska. They still live on those lands. The majority of them are clustered around Santee, Niobrara, and Lych, Nebraska. Much of the allotted land later was lost to Ponca owners by the sales they were allowed to make under the Allotment Act.

When the Poncas returned to the north, the government did not reestablish their old agency. For one thing, they were not located close enough to the old site to make it feasible; and for another, there was no longer enough of them in the north to justify maintaining a separate agency system. Thus, in 1881, they were placed under the Santee Agency in Nebraska and remained under that jurisdiction until 1917. In that year, their records and jurisdiction were transferred to the Yankton Agency located on the east side of the Missouri River at Greenwood, South Dakota. The Poncas and Yanktons had always been fairly friendly, and there was some intermarriage between them. By 1917, the tribal relations were very good. Yet, it was inconvenient for the Poncas to travel to the Yankton Agency. So, in 1933, they were placed under the jurisdiction of the Winnebago Agency adjacent to the Santee Agency in Nebraska. There they remained until the 1950's, when government control and supervision over the Northern Poncas ended. The 1950's was the period of termination. Mostly unjustified, in the case of the Northern Poncas, termination may have been a rational step. By that time, there were so few of them living under a reservation system that it no longer seemed worthwhile for the government to continue the relationship on a formal basis. Nonetheless, this decision would be questioned in later years by the remaining Northern Ponca.

Today, it is very doubtful that there are any full-blooded Northern Poncas remaining. They have intermarried extensively with the Santee Dakota, the Yankton Dakota, and the whites. Much of their old way of life has been forgotten. The old ceremonies and the old religion are seldom, if ever, practiced. Their new way of life tends to be more individualistic than tribal, and some would argue that it is impossible to speak of the Northern Ponca as a tribe any longer. Yet, the people do remain conscious of being Ponca and are proud of it. As long as that consciousness and pride remains, there will be a Northern branch of the Ponca people, no matter how few their numbers or how mingled their blood.

The security of the Poncas and their neighbors is constantly being threatened by the changes wrought in the Missouri River by the dam system which was constructed following World War II. Because of the Lewis and Clark Lake, which is formed by the Gavin's Point Dam, the silt and sediment of the Niobrara can no longer be swept away by the power of the Missouri and it settles at the mouths of the Ponca Creek and the Niobrara. The waters rise, and marshlands increase. The town of Niobrara, where many of the Northern Poncas live, is being rebuilt on a different site. The old village can no longer be seen. Many of the famous landmarks of the area are either under water or disintegrating. Maiden's Leap, east of Niobrara, is crumbling into the lake. Nor is it possible to locate Lewis and Clark Point any longer; it is under water. All of the old fields that once sustained the tribe are innundated. Yet, the people remain. They survive.

THE FUTURE

The Poncas are an old people, and a people who have suffered many things. They are a people of tradition who prefer to follow old ways as much as possible. They prefer the ancient dances to the new, the communal way of living to the individual, and they struggle to keep their clans alive by altering their functions, if not their basic purposes and organization. They are a people whose future is uncertain, and this causes them great concern.

One of the things that deeply troubles the older generation is the tribe's failure to retain its language. Language has always been, and will always be, a distinguishing mark of a separate and individual people. It expresses many things beyond mere communication. Language can hold the very soul of a people, and yet their innermost thoughts and concepts can never be held inviolate in a language other than their own. The Poncas worry because the younger generation is learning English and not Ponca. They want their children to be proficient in the use of English, but they also want them to retain their own language. No solution has as yet been found for this dilemma. The older generation, for the first time, is having difficulty transmitting the language to the youth, so many suggest that it will be necessary to create a system of formal education wherein the Ponca language is taught in a school or schools. This may be the solution for the future, but at present there are no programs for teaching the language in any of the schools that Ponca students attend. Many people feel that this is of the highest priority and must be one of the waves of the future.

Education in general is an area of concern for the leadership of the Ponca people. They are troubled

SILHOUETTED AGAINST AN AZURE SKY, this modern oil refinery occupies land that was once a part of the Ponca Indian Nation.

about high dropout rates in grade school and high school. There is special concern because they have not as yet produced a very large class of people with competence in the various fields of higher education and technology. In addition, they want everyone to have whatever education can offer in the way of a vocation. They feel that they need their people in everything from automotive mechanics to the practice of medicine, and they are working very hard to achieve this. Yet, education is slow; it takes decades before any newborn baby becomes a doctor, or a lawyer, or a professor. The Poncas have, and will continue to have, persistence in seeing that this goal is realized.

A more practical consideration is the continuing loss of the land base. As time goes on, more and more of the individual Poncas are selling their allotments and are usually selling them to white men. This is disastrous to a land base that has already been so terribly decimated, and, should it continue, the Poncas could conceivably end up as a landless tribe with no firm base on their Mother Earth. They see, as a solution to this problem, a massive program of land purchases by the tribe itself. The tribe, unfortunately, lacks the capital to do this and has had difficulty finding outside sources of funding. Because the Poncas do not have a recognized reservation as such, they are not eligible for the federal programs for the repurchase of land. As they have few assets that can serve as collateral, they also have difficulty trying to obtain funds from private sources. Unless something changes, they feel they will untimately find themselves at a dead end. To them, the most obvious solution is the reacquisition of reservation status from the federal government, which would make them eligible for grants, loans, and the like in a number of areas now denied them. They are working for this, but the inscrutable aims of a distant Congress and a scattered bureaucracy have so far foiled their efforts. They intend to continue until success is theirs, and their future on Mother Earth is assured.

The Poncas also worry much about the health of their people. They are forced to seek care at the Public Health facilities in Pawnee City, Oklahoma. This is at least sixty miles away, and sixty miles can be a death sentence to a man suffering from a heart attack. They have now started to build a new clinic, which will help. They likewise have a mobile dental unit, from which they expect great things. Yet, medical care falls very short of the ideal, and more facilities will be needed nearer to the people themselves, before anyone can begin to say that the Poncas have adequate health care. This is a problem that can and probably will be overcome, for the Poncas and their leaders are working very hard to find solutions.

On a long-range basis, the major problem of the Poncas is very simply the survival of themselves as a people. There are very few full-blooded Poncas alive at this time. Logic dictates that the blood lines of the tribe will be increasingly diluted by intermarriage with other Indians and other races. There is no logical way that this can be stopped, for no one can pass a rule against marriage. Yet, it is nevertheless a concern, albeit a long-range one. It is possible that a tribe could intermarry itself totally out of existence. The Poncas have no intention of allowing this to happen. They feel that as long as there are people who consider themselves to be Poncas, who can speak the language, who can relate to the tribe's history and traditions, their people will live.

The future of the Ponca people is shrouded in questions and in hazards. They have always been a great people, but they are small in numbers and scattered in habitat. They do not view their own future with any lack of hope, but rather with a sense of progress and improvement. The Poncas feel that they are moving towards a brighter world based on the older one. Who is to deny them? They have shown courage and tenacity in the past. They show it in the present, and they will unquestionably show it in the future. They are a nation that has learned the arts of survival and believe that they will survive into a future that will be better for them and for their children.

SUGGESTED READINGS

The books cited below include some of the published works on the history of the Poncas. This bibliography should offer a suitable beginning for the reader who desires to discover more about the subject. There are, of course, other excellent sources, which are available in most libraries.

DORSEY, JAMES OWEN. *Omaha and Ponca Letters.* Smithsonian Institution, Bureau of Ethnology. J. W. Powell, Director. Washington, D.C.: Government Printing Office, 1891.

This work involves a study of the Omaha and Ponca language through careful analysis and translations. It will probably appeal more to the specialist than the layman.

ENGLAND, GEORGE MILLER. "The Great Ranches: The Millers and the 101 Ranch" in *The Last Run: Kay County, Oklahoma, 1893.* Ponca City, Oklahoma: privately printed, 1939.

This brief account tells of the Miller Brothers, who from 1892 on managed to build a large cattle ranch by leasing and purchasing the lands of the Poncas and surrounding tribes. They also joined E. W. Marland to found an oil company. In 1931, because of a series of financial disasters, the ranch was liquidated. The government took it over and distributed the lands to needy Indians.

FOREMAN, GRANT. *The Last Trek of the Indians.* Chicago: University of Chicago Press, 1946.

Contains a balanced and scholarly treatment of the Ponca problems with the federal government.

HOWARD, JAMES H. *The Ponca Tribe.* Smithsonian Institution, Bureau of American Ethnology, Bulletin 195. Washington, D.C.: U.S. Government Printing Office, 1965.

This is the only overall work on the Poncas and is a valuable and interesting contribution.

JACKSON, HELEN HUNT. *A Century of Dishonor.* Reprint. New York: Harper and Row, 1965.

Contains a spirited account of the Ponca difficulties with the United States government from one who was deeply involved in the struggle.

MATHEWS, JOHN JOSEPH. *Life and Death of an Oilman: The Career of E. W. Marland.* Norman, Oklahoma: University of Oklahoma Press, 1951.

The story of a colorful entrepreneur, who struck oil on the lands surrounding Ponca City, Oklahoma at the turn of the century. Although he eventually fell on hard times, he still managed to live in luxury most of his life and became a Representative from and Governor of Oklahoma.

SKINNER, ALANSON. *Medicine Ceremony of the Meno-mini, Iowa, and Wahpeton Dakota, with Notes on the Ceremonies Among the Ponca, Bungi, Ojibwa, and Potawatomi* in *Indian Notes and Monographs*, Volume IV. New York: Museum of the American Indian, Heye Foundation, 1920.

There is a brief but useful section devoted to the Ponca Pebble Ceremony.

SKINNER, ALANSON. *Societies of the Iowa, Kansas, and Ponca Indians* in *Anthropological Papers of the American Museum of Natural History*, Volume XI, Part IX. New York, 1915.

A detailed account of the political, social, and ceremonial organization of the Iowa, Kansa, and Ponca Indians.

TIBBLES, HENRY THOMAS. *The Ponca Chiefs*. Boston: Lockwood, Brooks and Company, 1880.

A useful work written by a fiery reformer, who worked hard to help the Poncas in their difficulties with the federal government.

WELSH, WILLIAM. *Report on the Sioux and Ponka Indians on the Missouri River*. Washington, D.C.: Government Printing Office, 1872.

A valuable report providing insight into the condition of the Sioux and Poncas.

WELSH, WILLIAM. *Sioux and Ponca Indians: Reports to the Missionary Organizations of the Protestant Episcopal Church and the Secretary of the Interior on Indian Civilization.* Philadelphia: M'Calla and Stavely, 1870.

An interesting report based upon the experiences, perspective, and biases of one who knew the Poncas well.

WILL, GEORGE F. and GEORGE E. HYDE. *Corn Among the Indians.* Lincoln, Nebraska: University of Nebraska Press, 1917.

A detailed treatment of the various roles corn played in the lives of the Upper Missouri Indians, including the Poncas.

WILSON, DOROTHY CLARKE. *Bright Eyes: The Story of Susette LaFlesche, an Omaha Indian.* New York: McGraw-Hill Book Company, 1974.

A fascinating saga about a woman who used her eloquence and knowledge successfully to persuade the United States government to provide a measure of justice and more suitable laws for the Poncas and Omahas.

ZIMMERMAN, C. L. *White Eagle: Chief of the Poncas.* Harrisburg, Pennsylvania: The Telegraph Press, 1941.

Not only deals with the life of White Eagle but also is an excellent source for discovering many aspects of Ponca life and history. In addition, it contains an interesting section on Zimmerman's experiences as a physician among the Poncas.

THE AUTHORS

 JOSEPH H. CASH is Duke Research Professor of History at the University of South Dakota, Director of the American Indian Research Project and the South Dakota Oral History Project. He taught at Eastern Montana College before coming to the University of South Dakota. A native of South Dakota, Professor Cash earned his B.A. and M.A. degrees from the University of South Dakota, and the Ph.D. from the University of Iowa. He has conducted and directed oral history among a great many of the Northern Plains tribes, and has published on both Indian history and mining history.

GERALD W. WOLFF is Associate Professor of History at the University of South Dakota. He taught at California State University at Long Beach prior to assuming his present position. A native of Ohio, Professor Wolff has the B.S. and M.A. degrees from Bowling Green University, and the Ph.D. from the University of Iowa. A specialist in Nineteenth Century American History, he has published numbers of articles in professional journals. Professor Wolff has interviewed American Indians about their history for the American Indian Research Project at the University of South Dakota, and is presently working on several manuscripts.